party games

Jane Kemp and Clare Walters

hamlyn

First published in Great Britain
in 2003 by Hamlyn, a division of
Octopus Publishing Group Ltd
2–4 Heron Quays, London E14 4JP

ISBN 0 600 60694 5
EAN 9780600606949

A CIP catalogue record for this book
is available from the British Library

Printed and bound in China

10 9 8 7 6 5 4 3 2

contents

how to use this book

We all remember great birthday parties from when we were little. Your child's party can be just as much fun if you use this book to help you plan it.

If you're just beginning to think about your child's party, read Chapter One. This will give you plenty of ideas about the main decisions you'll need to make before you even get round to choosing the games. For instance, do you want a big gathering with lots of children and noise, or would you prefer a more intimate best friends get-together? Will you be able to call on lots of adult helpers for lively team games, or would it be better to focus on more easily contained games where supervision will be simpler? Other key things you'll need to think about are also in this chapter, such as venues, themes, timings, music and the all-important food.

Finally, if you are giving a party for babies or toddlers, read Chapter Seven. This has practical ideas for parties for pre-school children, with suggested lists of games and activities appropriate for each age group (cross-referenced to the chapters), as well as hints and tips on making the party a memorable success.

Lastly, remember to enjoy the party yourself. It's a celebration after all, and your children will enjoy it much more if they see you relaxed and happy. Have fun!

You may already know what sort of party you're going to have and just want to find some suitable games to play. If so, browse through Chapters Two to Six to make a selection that would suit your child's age and interests. Each of these chapters has a particular theme – musical, circle, lively, quiet and chasing games – so for a shy child you might choose circle and quiet games, while for a more active one you might select the lively and chasing games. For each game, you will see the suggested age range, what props you'll need and whether it requires music. Make a list of the games (together with their props) that you've chosen and put them in the order in which you want to play them. Then mark the appropriate pages of this book using sticky notes with numbers in order at the top so you can easily find the games.

planning a party

SECRETS OF SUCCESS

The simple secret of a successful party is to be well prepared. If you know what you're going to do, and plan carefully, the children will have a good time and leave happy. Knowing that everything is in hand helps you to relax, and that rubs off on the children too, who will feel they're in safe hands.

invitations

Two to three weeks before the party, you'll need to send out written invitations. They will need to say the child's name and which birthday it is, the address, the phone number, the date and start and finish times of the party. If you're having a themed party, your invitation should make clear whether the guest needs to dress up for this or whether you'll be providing props. You may also need a small map if you're inviting children whose parents haven't been to your home before.

Who's coming?
Busy parents often forget to respond to invitations, especially when they have more than one child. If you need to confirm numbers, ask them to reply by a certain date.

how many helpers?

It's unrealistic to think that you can manage a party entirely on your own – by the end you'll be exhausted, and it could be unsafe if you need to leave the children unsupervised while you deal with a problem. Generally speaking, you'll need more helpers for younger children as they might be shy and need extra encouragement to join in games, as well as more practical help with going to the toilet and washing their hands. If you're having a party for under-threes, you'll need to ask the parents to stay on, anyway, and you may still need to do this for some under-fours.

Parties for older children also need helpers. If there's an accident, even something as simple as a spilt drink, you'll need someone to help sort the child out while you continue to entertain the other guests. Also, it can be very helpful to have someone to set out the party tea while you organize the games. Even if you have an entertainer, you'll still need help before and after the show. As a guideline, think about having one adult to every four children.

indoors or outdoors?

Most of the games in this book can be played successfully either indoors or outdoors. If you're trusting the weather and planning an outdoor party, make sure you have an alternative venue to fall back on if the weather fails.

Things to think about for an indoor party:

- Have you got enough space to play some lively games?

- Are there things you should put away to avoid them being broken accidentally?

- Are there rooms you want to keep out of bounds?

- If you want them to take their shoes off, have you got somewhere to store them? (A big cardboard box would be ideal.)

Things to think about for an outdoor party:

- Have you fenced off any ponds?

- Is the outdoor area secure and will you be able to keep your eye on all the children at once?

- Will you be able to transport all the food and props to the party area easily?

- Will you need to take hand-wipes and bottles of water for quick clean-ups?

a party away from home

If you'd prefer to contain the party noise and mess somewhere other than your own home, there are plenty of suitable venues that cater for parties. The cost can often be high if you're inviting large numbers because you're likely to be charged per child, and there may be a minimum charge, even if you have fewer children. However, you may feel it's worth it as it gives the children extra space, and you will come back to a clean home.

Some places provide a room and basic kitchen facilities; others organize games, activities and the party tea. Make sure you're clear about what's on offer before booking. For example, a two-hour party at a leisure centre may only include one hour's entertainment – the rest of the time it's up to you to keep the children happy. Check what you'll need to bring, such as party hats, party bags and balloons.

Places to think about:

- A village or church hall can usually be hired by the hour. You'll need to clear up after.

- A leisure centre may offer a choice of activity parties such as swimming, roller-skating, football or soft play. For young children you'll need to check how many adults per child are required. Ask if catering facilities are provided.

- A restaurant or family pub. Many chains offer organized parties with food included.

- Bowling alley. Six-year-olds and over will enjoy going bowling.

- Farm. Some visitor farms offer parties, although you'll probably need to bring food. Good hygiene will be essential.

Present know-how
If you have a lot of children coming to the party, it's best to put all the presents aside for your child to open when the party's over. Otherwise it could take ages to open them all and your child will want to play with them at once. Keep a list of who's given what for thank yous later.

budgeting

Parties can cost a lot of money, but they don't have to. You can economize by:

- Having the party at home.

- Making all your own food, including the cake.

- Keeping party bags simple. A home-made biscuit with the child's initial on will be just as popular (if not more so) than a fancy toy.

- Restricting numbers. A party with just a small number of close friends is often more successful than a party where the whole class is invited.

- Making your own entertainment with party games and activities rather than hiring an entertainer – this book has all the ideas you'll need.

welcome to the party

Some lively music and a bunch of bright helium balloons with long strings will break the ice immediately as the party guests arrive. You will need to gather the balloons together in one corner once you start the games. Make sure you have one for each child and a few spare in case any pop. At the end of the party, each child can take one home.

suitable themes

Themed parties are often popular, especially if your child is currently going through a phase of liking particular games or characters. You can keep the theme very simple, with just a few eye patches for pirates for example, or you can go to town and theme everything from the invitations to napkins. Here are some possible ideas (right).

For mixed parties:
- Fancy dress
- Animals
- Circus characters and animals
- Fairytale characters
- Pop stars
- Television and film characters
- Witches and wizards
- Sun, moon and stars

For boys:
- Pirates
- Explorers
- Aliens
- Cowboys

For girls:
- Fairies
- Princesses
- Dancers
- Mermaids

Your party countdown planner

**Two to
three weeks before** Send out the invitations.

One week before Check who's replied and chase up any you've not heard from. Check in advance if any guests have any special food requirements.

Three days before Buy any props, such as balloons, streamers, paper tablecloth, party cups and plates or party food boxes, if using (see page 63), napkins, party bags and items to put in them and little presents for prizes.

Two days before Sort out what games you'll play. If you like, write them on small cards that you can shuffle around to suit the mood of the party. Alternatively, just make a list to keep close at hand.

One day before

Buy the food and make the cake if you're doing it yourself (don't forget drinks and snacks for your adult helpers). Check the props again and tidy away any ornaments or items you don't want damaged. Make sure you have enough music – and a working CD or cassette player!

On the day

Prepare fresh food for the party tea (keep cool if necessary). Collect helium balloons or inflate party balloons, if you are using them. Pack food and props if you are having a party away from home.

food

From a surprisingly early age, children have strong ideas about what they expect to eat at a party tea. Basically the food is split into four key areas:
- Savoury
- Sweet
- Drinks
- The all-important cake

Try to encourage everyone to have something savoury before they tuck into the sweet treats. Also check that every child has had enough to drink as they do get hot and thirsty when they've been playing lively games. Younger children, especially, may be too shy to ask for a drink, even though they need one (the same goes for visits to the toilet).

Savoury food
Children love to choose their own selection of items from an array of different plates. Try some of the suggestions below:

- Sandwiches – a party basic that can be made much more appealing by being cut into tiny triangles or shapes with food cutters. Offer a selection of fillings (grated cheese, yeast extract, ham, tomato, tuna, cucumber) so there's something for everyone. Make sure the bread is really soft and fresh, don't overfill the sandwich – and cut the crusts off.

- Pizza fingers – cut a pizza into manageable sections that children can eat easily with their fingers. It's usually best to stick to the basic cheese and tomato or ham varieties.

Tidy-up time
Have lots of rubbish bags ready for wrapping paper, paper plates and napkins, and food packaging.

- Tiny quiches and little scotch eggs – bite-sized are best.

- Mini sausages or sausage rolls – again, the smaller the better.

- Buttered finger rolls – for those children who don't like any of the sandwich fillings (there are bound to be some).

- Mini vegetables and dips – cut carrots, cucumber, red and yellow peppers into sticks, add a few cherry tomatoes and offer them with some hummus or cream cheese for dips.

- Breadsticks, cheese straws and mini cheese biscuits – easy to eat and filling.

- Cheese and pineapple on cocktail sticks (older children only) – always popular!

- Crisps and potato rings.

Sweet food

The best bit for most children! Make portions small so they can try as much as they want.

- Biscuits – chocolate fingers, pink wafers, jam sandwiches and iced rings usually hit the spot with most children.

- Cakes – popular choices include wrapped chocolate mini rolls (one for each child), tiny fairy cakes cooked in paper cases with a chocolate button to decorate, and chocolate-covered marshmallows.

Drinks

- Juice – apple, orange and cranberry; always dilute well.

- Squashes – orange, lemon, strawberry or blackcurrant.

- Water – the best thirst-quencher of all.

- Fizzy drinks – hold these back until everyone has quenched their thirst with watery drinks, and keep quantities small.

The cake

The cake is the highlight of the birthday tea, although by the time it's brought out the children are often so full that they can't actually manage any. However, they'll love to take a slice home wrapped in a napkin as part of their goody bag. (You may like to allow a slice for brothers and sisters too, if it's a big cake.)

There are lots of themed cakes you can buy, but you can also buy a simple sponge cake to customize for your child. Use ready-made icing and icing pens to decorate. Lots of sweets on the top helps make it a hit!

Here are some easy-to-prepare cake ideas:

- Caterpillar – made from a wavy row of chocolate-covered marshmallows. Make a face and decorate the body with sweets, and use chocolate sticks for antennae and legs.

- Train – use a whole Swiss roll for the engine, then two carriages made from a second one, cut in half horizontally. You can load the carriages with sweets for cargo. Finish the train with funnels and wheels made from mini rolls and tracks made from chocolate sticks.

- Castle – add ice-cream cone 'turrets' to the corners of a square cake to make a fairytale castle.

- Treasure box – cut a square cake in half horizontally and stand one half upright behind the other. Cover with chocolate icing. When it's dry, pile gold and silver chocolate coins inside the 'casket' as treasure.

Birthday Cake Candles
Don't forget to have the right number of candles and a supply of matches, but supervise your child very closely as he blows them out, especially if any of the children have long hair and are leaning forward to help.

To add drama, you may want to draw the curtains and turn off the light before bringing in the cake, but give the children warning that this is going to happen so that no one gets frightened. It's nice to start the children singing '*Happy Birthday*' as the cake appears.

Buy ordinary cake candles for young children, rather than the trick ones which re-light, as this is not only confusing for little ones but could also be dangerous.

Food essentials
Make sure that you are aware of any child's particular food requirements, for example, if they are vegetarian or allergic to any foods, such as nuts.

Your party timetable

3.00–3.15pm

Guests arrive. Make a note of each child's phone number before parents leave, just in case you need to contact them.

3.15–3.45pm

Mix of lively and quiet games (see pages 44–55 and 56–67).

3.45–4.00pm

Play a one-by-one 'out' game so that the children can visit the toilet and wash their hands before tea (see page 25).

Balance the fun
Alternate lively games with sitting-down games to give the party a comfortable balance. You'll probably find that lively games are over fairly quickly, while sitting-down games can last for quite a while.

4.00–4.30pm   The party tea with birthday
cake, candles and song.

4.30–5.00pm   Quiet games followed by
a lively circle game to end
(see pages 32–43).

5.00pm   Parents arrive. If you want,
offer them a drink while the
children have free play or
watch a video.

musical games

GETTING IT RIGHT

Everyone loves musical games and all you need is a simple cassette or CD player – or your own voice. The tips below will help the games go with a swing:

- Instrumental music works better than vocal music.

- Choose music with a fast beat.

- Press the 'pause' rather than the 'stop' button on a cassette player, so the children don't have to wait too long between the parts of the game.

- If the children are getting too loud, turn the music down a little so they have to make less noise in order to hear the instructions for the game.

- Sometimes little children enjoy simply sitting together and singing favourite nursery rhymes, so don't feel you have to have rules and prizes for everything.

row the boat
age 1+
props none
music you sing

This simple game can be enjoyed even by very young children. It's played in pairs with the two partners sitting opposite each other. For babies, the parent sits opposite; older children can sit together. Rock backwards and forwards holding hands as you sing the words:

Row, row, row your boat,
Gently down the stream.
Merrily, merrily,
merrily, merrily,
Life is but a dream.

Play tip
Allow enough space so that pairs don't bump into each other as they rock backwards.

Quiet corner
Put a few books on a sofa nearby for a shy child to look at quietly while the others play. Say, 'Why don't you sit here until you're ready to join in.' The less fuss you make, the more likely they are to want to play.

if you're happy and you know it

age 1+
props none
music you sing

Children love to know they can do something well and this game is something everyone can succeed at. Sing the verse below, matching the actions to the words, and then changing them with each verse. You can follow the ones suggested below or make up your own.

If you're happy and you know it, clap your hands.
(CLAP, CLAP)
If you're happy and you know it, clap your hands.
(CLAP, CLAP)
If you're happy and you know it, then you surely want to show it, If you're happy and you know it, clap your hands.
(CLAP, CLAP)

For the final verse, shout, *'WE ARE!'*

Other actions to try:
● Stamp your feet
● Nod your head
● Turn around
● Jump up and down

Play tip
If you know your child has just mastered a new skill, be sure to include it on the list!

happy birthday animals

age 2+
props none
music you sing

Divide the children into four groups, naming them dogs, cats, horses or pigs. They have to pretend to be the animals as you sing *Happy Birthday To You.* When it comes to *'Happy Birthday dear...'*, you say an animal name – *'Happy Birthday dear Dogs'*, for example, and all the 'dogs' then bark as loud as they can. Finish the game by singing, *'Happy Birthday EVERYONE'*, when all the children make their animals noises together.

Play tip
Make sure each animal group has at least one turn on their own before you finish the game with the whole group making their noises together.

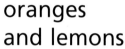

'*Oranges and lemons,*'
say the bells of St Clement's.
'*I owe you five farthings,*'
say the bells of St Martin's.
'*When will you pay me?*'
say the bells of Old Bailey.
'*When I grow rich,*'
say the bells of Shoreditch.
'*When will that be?*'
say the bells of Stepney.
'*I do not know,*'
says the great bell of Bow.

oranges and lemons

age 3+
props paper party hats
music you sing

This new version of an old favourite (based on bells in famous London churches) has a happier ending than the traditional head chopping. Two adults form an arch with their arms, holding a party hat above them. The children line up, and pass through the arch one at a time as you sing the words:

(Sing this slowly.)
Here comes a candle to light you to bed.
(Lift the crown up and down.)
Here comes a hat to wear on your head.
Not too big, and not too tight,
Here's the hat that looks just right!
(You put a paper hat on the child's head and they sit out, wearing it.)

Play tip
Make sure you have enough paper hats to hand and plenty of extras in case any get damaged.

musical bumps
age 3+
props none
music yes

The children all dance to the music but when it stops they sit down as fast as possible on the floor. The last one to bump down is out each time and can join the grown-ups in being a judge (you may also need to offer a small consolation sweet). The last child left is the winner.

Play tip
You can play this with two-year-olds, but be prepared to give them a lot of reminders as to how the game works.

musical statues
age 4+
props none
music yes

As with Musical Bumps, the children all dance to music. But instead of sitting down when the music stops, they have to stand as still as they can. If anyone wobbles, they're 'out'.

Play tip
Choose some really bouncy music to encourage the children to dance in a lively way.

musical cushions
age 5+
props a cushion for every child
music yes

Lay two rows of cushions on the floor. When the music starts, the children march round the cushions. When the music stops, they have to sit down on a cushion as quickly as possible. Have a cushion for each child for the first round, then remove one for the second round. The child who doesn't get a cushion is 'out'. Continue removing the cushions until there is only one child left – the winner.

Play tip
Keep all the removed cushions away from the children who are 'out' or you could find you have a cushion fight on your hands.

Prizes
Have a small prize for each winner. Good prizes for over-threes are boxes of crayons, transfers, stickers, chalks, mini jigsaws, modelling clay or small toys. For under-threes, prizes aren't really necessary – they'll be happy with a hug and a clap.

five currant buns

age 2+
props none
music you sing

A good game for playing with a small group of young children. The birthday child is the 'boy' or 'girl', and stands on one side of the room. All the others are 'buns', and stand on the opposite side of the room. Sing the verse and mime the actions, and encourage the children to join in:

*Five currant buns
in the baker's shop,*
(Hold up right number of fingers.)
*Round and fat
with some sugar on the top.*
(Make a circle with your hands and pat your head for the sugar.)
Along came a boy/girl with a penny one day,
(Walk your fingers along as the birthday child comes in to the 'shop'.)
*Bought a currant bun
and took it right away.*
(The birthday child leads one of the 'buns' away from the shop to his side of the room.)

Continue with four, three, two, and one currant bun, until the final verse:

*No currant buns in the baker's shop,
Round and fat with some sugar on the top.
Along came a boy/girl with a penny one day,
But there were NO currant buns for him/her to take away!*
(The children shake their heads and shout out the last line.)

Play tip

If you have more than six children at the party you can simply increase the number of buns, but remember the game will take slightly longer.

the wheels on the bus

age 1+
props none
music you sing

This is ideal for very young children but you'll be surprised how much the older ones enjoy it, too. The children sit down and mime the appropriate actions to the song below:

The wheels on the bus
go round and round,
round and round,
round and round.
The wheels on the bus
go round and round,
all day long.
(Make large circles at your sides with your hands.)

Other words and actions:
- *The windscreen wipers go swish, swish, swish.* (Move your arms from left to right.)
- *The people on the bus bounce up and down.* (Bounce up and down.)
- *The mums on the bus go chatter, chatter, chatter.* (Make your hands 'chatter'.)
- *The babies on the bus go waa, waa, waa.* (Pretend to rub your eyes and cry.)

Play tip
Do the actions yourself to show the younger ones how to do them.

how do I dance?

age 2+
props none
music you sing

Put on some music so the children can enjoy a dance. Stop the music and say, 'How do we dance? We dance by shaking our arms!' Put the music back on and dance in that way. The next time you stop the music suggest a new way to dance, such as 'waving our hands in the air', 'turning around', 'bending our knees', 'wiggling our elbows' or 'clapping our hands'.

Play tip
Alternate lively actions with gentle ones, so the game doesn't get too fast and furious.

Won't play?
There's often a child who doesn't want to join in, either because they're shy or don't like the game. You could try whispering, 'If you join in you might win a prize!' – it's amazing how effective this can be. Or ask if they'd like to play the game with a partner.

hokey cokey

age 3+
props none
music you sing

Stand in a circle. For the first two
lines of the song, follow the
actions suggested by the words.
For the 'Hokey Cokey', you join
your hands and rock them from
side to side, then turn around.
For the chorus, everyone holds
hands and dances in and out of
the centre three times then bend
their knees, stretch their arms
and shout out the final line.

You put your right arm in,
your right arm out,
In, out, in, out,
shake it all about.
You do the Hokey Cokey
and you turn around.
That's what it's all about.

Chorus:
Oh, oh, the Hokey Cokey!,
Oh, oh, the Hokey Cokey!,
Oh, oh, the Hokey Cokey!,
Knees bend, arms stretch,
Ra, ra, ra!

Other verses:
• *Right leg in*
• *Left arm in*
• *Left leg in*
• *Whole self in*

Play tip
Intersperse some adults among the
children so that they don't all rush
into the centre and bump heads.

Time for tea
Musical games where children are
'out' on a one-by-one basis can be a
handy device for getting everyone's
hands washed before sitting down to
tea. You'll need some adults on
standby to help with this.

living piano

age 5+
props none
music no

This is a game for children who enjoy music and singing. Divide them into pairs and give each pair in turn a different note from a simple musical scale to sing. (Sing it first and then get them to sing it back to you.) The children are now part of a 'living piano'.

Then you act as the 'piano player' – when you point at a pair of children, they sing their note. (Being in pairs helps give the children confidence, but if they are enjoying this game you could give some of them notes to sing individually.)

Then see if they can sing a scale, singing up and then back down again. If the children are OK with scales, try making simple tunes like *Baa, Baa Black Sheep* (eight notes) or *Twinkle, Twinkle Little Star* (six notes). To end the game, have a glorious finale where everyone sings their notes as loudly as they possibly can!

Play tip

Younger children may enjoy a variation on this game, where each pair of children sing an individual word from a well-known song, such as *Ten Green Bottles*.

dressing-up dance

age 3+
props A paper party hat, an eye mask or pirate patch, a badge and a sticker for each child.
music lively dance music

Everyone starts dancing to the music. The dressing-up props are distributed evenly round the outside of the room. When the music stops, the children stand still until you tell them which item you want them to fetch: 'Everyone take... a HAT!', at which point they all hunt for a hat and put it on. When everyone is wearing a hat, the music starts again and they dance around until it's time to find the next item, e.g. a mask, sticker or badge. Cheap jewellery could be added to the dressing-up pile for girls; fake moustaches or medals would be good for boys.

Play tip
To introduce the children to each other, get them to find and put on stickers with their names.

what's the sound?

age 4+
props simple musical instruments
music no

Collect a selection of noisy musical instruments, for example, a party squeaker, recorder, toy drum, kazoo, rattle, tambourine, triangle or mini keyboard. Alternatively, you can make your own musical 'instruments' at home – two saucepan lids to bang together like cymbals, a plastic pot with a lid half filled with dried lentils for a shaker or a piece of paper folded over a comb. Demonstrate the instruments to the children before you start, and tell them what each one is called. Then get the children to sit in front of a screen or the sofa, and hide behind it with your noisy toys. Play a sound on one instrument, and ask the children to shout out what they think it is. Everyone gets a sweet as a prize once all the sounds have been identified.

Play tip
An extra adult helper is essential for this game as you won't be able to supervise from your hiding place.

nursery rhyme pop stars

age 3+
props pretend microphone
music some well-known nursery rhymes

This is a chance for the more confident guests at your party to shine. Sit the children in a group in front of you and start the game by asking, 'Does anyone here know a song called *Humpty Dumpty*?' The children will probably answer, 'Yes!' at which point you say, 'Can anyone here sing *Humpty Dumpty* – all on their own?' Hopefully you'll get another yes and then you can invite the child to come to the front, saying, 'OK, come out to be our first pop star, then!' The 'star' then takes the pretend microphone and sings the song to the others. When he's finished, everyone gives him a big clap.

Other good songs to suggest include: *Rock A Bye Baby*, *Twinkle Twinkle Little Star*, *I'm A Little Teapot* and *Incy Wincy Spider*; or popular TV theme tunes such as *Barney* or *Bob the Builder*.

Play tip
To get the game going you may want to plant an older child at the party who is willing to get up and sing first.

CHAPTER 3

circle games

SECRETS OF SUCCESS

Most of these games work both indoors or out, but make sure the ground isn't damp if the children are sitting down.

- Move furniture to the edges of the room before the party, to allow space to make a circle.

- If indoors, get children to take their shoes off so that no one gets hurt if kicked accidentally.

- Make sure that no one is sitting behind a door, otherwise they could get bumped.

- Some games require a child to be blindfolded. Always check that they are happy about this. They may prefer just to shut their eyes tightly instead.

- If you have a mixed party of boys and girls, try to alternate them around the circle.

- For a large or very lively group, mix a few adult helpers in.

weird whispers

age 4+
props none
music no

Start this game by whispering a silly sentence to the first child. That child then passes the whisper on to the child sitting next to her in the circle. The whisper continues until it gets back to the beginning, at which point the last child says the sentence out loud. Compare what they say to the sentence the game began with.

Sentences to try:
- Ten tiny toes tiptoed to bed
- Sweet Suzie sews socks for sailors
- Peter's pocket was packed with plums
- Crazy cats cry at crows

Play tip
It's best to make up the sentences yourself to avoid putting a child on the spot.

the farmer's in his den

age 2+
props none
music you sing

The children stand in a ring holding hands. One child is selected to be the farmer and stands in the middle. Everyone then sings the song. On the second verse the farmer chooses a child from the circle to join him as his wife. With each new verse the last child to be selected chooses another child to join the group in the middle. The last child is the 'bone', and becomes the next farmer.

The farmer's in his den,
the farmer's in his den,
Eee, aye, eee, aye,
the farmer's in his den.

Other verses:
- *The farmer wants a wife*
- *The wife wants a child*
- *The child wants a nurse*
- *The nurse wants a dog*
- *The dog wants a bone*
- *We all clap the bone*

Play tip
If you've got a large group of children, the ones in the middle can join hands and go round in a smaller circle of their own.

clap my name

age 2+
props none
music no

This is a good game to introduce the children to each other at the start of the party. Go around the circle asking each child her name. When a child says her name, you then clap the syllables and get all the children to copy it. So, for example, if the child's name was Madeline, you'd clap three times as you said 'Ma-de-line!'.

Play tip
Taking turns around the circle, the older children could ask the person next to them their name and clap it out themselves.

story round

age 4+
props none
music no

Start a story off, for example, 'Once upon a time there was a little dog who got lost on his way home ...'. Then ask each child in turn to continue the story. You can bring it to an end once all the children have had a turn.

Play tip

Put out paper and colouring pens, and ask all the children to draw a picture illustrating the story they've invented together.

in and out the dusty bluebells

age 3+
props none
music you sing

One child is chosen to begin and the others join hands and form arches by raising their arms. The chosen child dances in and out of the 'bluebell' arches as everyone sings the verse. When she gets to the end of the first verse, she stands behind a child in the circle and taps them on the shoulder

Keep the adults happy

Don't forget that the adult helpers will get hungry and thirsty as well. Put out some suitable adult snacks and drinks, away from the main party tea table.

for the chorus. That child then stands in front of the first child, who holds her waist, and the two of them start weaving back through the bluebells again for a repeat of the verse. A new child joins the line for each chorus, until it all ends in mayhem.

In and out the dusty bluebells,
In and out the dusty bluebells,
In and out the dusty bluebells,
Who shall be my partner?

Chorus:
Tippy tippy tappy
on your shoulder,
Tippy tippy tappy
on your shoulder,
Tippy tippy tappy
on your shoulder,
You shall be my partner.

Play tip

For younger children or smaller party groups, you may prefer them to swap places instead of joining a long line, so that there is no more than one child 'weaving'.

lost letter

age 5+
props a 'letter'
music no

The children sit in a circle and one child is selected to 'send' the letter. This child walks around the outside saying the verse, with your help. At the end of the verse he drops the letter behind a child, who then jumps up and the two children race in opposite directions around the outside of the circle to get back to the empty space. Whoever gets there first sits down, and the other child starts the game again.

*I sent a letter to my love
and on the way I dropped it.
One of you has picked it up
and put it in your pocket.
It wasn't you, it wasn't you,
it ... was ... you!*

Play tip
Make sure there's enough space for the children to run around the outside of the circle without tripping over anyone or anything.

squeak, Piggy, squeak!

age 5+
props soft scarf, cushion
music no

For this game, the children sit in a circle. Choose one child to stand in the middle. Give him a cushion to hold and cover his eyes with a soft scarf, then turn him around and lead him to a child in the circle. He then puts the cushion on the child's lap and sits down, saying, 'Squeak, Piggy, squeak!'. The child has to 'oink' three times and the blindfolded child has to guess who it is. If he's right, the Piggy puts on the blindfold and has a turn; if he's wrong, he tries another child.

Play tip
If you'd prefer children not to sit on each other, you could play this game by tapping the shoulder of the child who has to squeak.

who's got the treasure?

age 5+
props a long circle of string with a ring or bead (the treasure) along it
music no

One child sits in the middle, while the others all sit in a circle, holding the string, passing the ring or bead (the treasure) secretly from hand to hand. When you call out 'Stop', the person in the middle has to try to guess who is holding the treasure. If she is right, she swaps places with the person holding the treasure; if she gets it wrong, the treasure continues to be passed round the circle.

Play tip
Have some real treasure to distribute at the end of the game, such as a bag of chocolate coins.

My turn!
Try to have a different child starting each game, so that one child doesn't dominate. Remember, even shy children may enjoy the thrill of being picked to go first.

who can build a tower?

age 1+
props cube-shaped building bricks, all the same size
music no

This game is ideal for even the youngest party guests, although mums will need to help a lot. Each child is given a brick. Start the game by putting a brick in the centre of the circle, then each child in turn adds a brick to help to build the tower until it topples down. The next child in the circle starts off the new tower. Build the excitement by counting out loud, and give a big clap to each toddler who successfully places a brick on the tower.

Play tip
Because this is a game for very young children, you don't need to offer prizes, but they may appreciate a little sweet or snack at the end for trying so hard.

Old MacDonald had a farm

age 2+
props none
music you sing

Give all the children an animal to be in the song, but choose one child to be Old MacDonald the farmer. He stands in the centre of the circle and they all sing the verse. When it comes to the animal name, all the children who are being sheep, for example, come into the middle of the circle with Old MacDonald, and only they can make the actual animal noises. At the end of the verse they go back to their places and a new set of children join the farmer with the next verse. For the final verse, everyone joins in making the animal noises.

Old MacDonald had a farm,
eee-aye-eee-aye-oh.
And on that farm he had some
sheep, eee-aye-eee-aye-oh.
With a baa-baa here
and a baa-baa there,
Here a baa, there a baa,
everywhere a baa-baa,
Old MacDonald had a farm,
eee-aye-eee-aye-oh.

Other verses:
- Cows (moo-moo)
- Hens (cluck-cluck)
- Horses (neigh-neigh)
- Dogs (woof-woof)
- Pigs (oink-oink)
- Cats (miaow-miaow)
- Ducks (quack-quack)
- Lots of animals (variety of sounds)

Play tip
Encourage the children to make really loud animal noises by making them yourself.

London Bridge is falling down

age 3+
props chocolate buttons and small sweets
music you sing

Two adults hold hands to form an arch. The children line up and pass under the arch as you sing the words. At the end of the verse, the adults 'capture' one of the children by bringing their arms down on either side of the child. One adult is called 'Sweets'; the other 'Chocolate'. One adult asks the child in a whisper, 'Sweets or Chocolate?'. The child whispers back their choice and is then directed to stand behind the appropriate adult. When all the children are lined up behind the adults, the Sweets team gets a small sweet each; the Chocolate team each get a chocolate button.

*London Bridge is falling down,
falling down, falling down.
London Bridge is falling down,
my fair lady!*

*Build it up with wood and clay,
wood and clay, wood and clay.
Build it up with wood and clay,
my fair lady.
Wood and clay will wash away,
wash away, wash away.
Wood and clay will wash away,
my fair lady.*

*Build it up with bricks and mortar,
bricks and mortar, bricks and mortar.
Build it up with bricks and mortar,
my fair lady.*

*Bricks and mortar will not stay,
will not stay, will not stay.
Bricks and mortar will not stay,
my fair lady.*

*Build it up with iron and steel,
iron and steel, iron and steel.
Build it up with iron and steel,
my fair lady.*

*Iron and steel will bend and
bow,
bend and bow, bend and bow.
Iron and steel will bend and
bow,
my fair lady.*

*Build it up with silver and gold,
silver and gold, silver and gold.
Build it up with silver and gold,
my fair lady.*

*Silver and gold will be stolen
away,
stolen away, stolen away.
Silver and gold will be stolen
away,
my fair lady.*

*But London Bridge is falling
down,
falling down, falling down.
London Bridge is falling down,
my FAIR LADY!*

Play tip
A tug of war between the two teams
is fun for older children but is
probably best played outside.

bish-bash saucepan

age 3+
props a blindfold, a large saucepan
and a wooden spoon
music no

Blindfold one child and sit her
down in the middle of the circle
on the floor holding a wooden
spoon. Then quietly place the
saucepan upside down in front
of her. She has to 'bash' about
with the spoon until she finds
the saucepan – and makes a good
crashing sound by hitting it. Once
she's found it, blindfold another
child and put the saucepan in a
different place.

Play tip
You could put more than one
saucepan down in the circle to make
it easier to find.

Calming down time
A sitting-down circle game can
be just what's needed if things
are getting a bit out of hand, as
it gathers all the children together
in one place and is much more
controlled than an energetic
running-about game.

here we go round the mulberry bush

age 2+
props none
music you sing

The children join hands and walk round in a circle as they sing the chorus below. Then they stand still for the verses and mime the actions suggested by the words.

Chorus:
Here we go round the mulberry bush, the mulberry bush, the mulberry bush.
Here we go round the mulberry bush, all on a summer's morning.

Verse:
This is the way we get out of bed, get out of bed, get out of bed.
This is the way we get out of bed, all on a summer's morning.

Other verses:
- *Wash out face*
- *Brush our teeth*
- *Comb our hair*
- *Put on our clothes*
- *Eat out breakfast*

Play tip
You can pick a theme that reflects your child's interests for the actions, such as football ('This is the way we save the goal') or ballet ('This is the way we point our toes').

pass the parcel

age 3+

props small present wrapped in several layers of paper. You may want to put a sweet or tiny toy between each layer.

music yes

The children sit in a circle and one child is given the parcel to start the game off. When the music is playing, the parcel must be passed from child to child; when it stops, the child holding the parcel can unwrap a single layer of paper and claim the sweet or toy, if there is one. The child unwrapping the last layer claims the prize. You can play this with younger children but wrap the layers very loosely and be prepared for some reluctant passers-on.

Play tip

Be sure to wrap the prize in at least the same number of layers as you have children at the party, so that every child gets a turn.

the chocolate game

age 4+

props chocolate buttons, hat, scarf, sunglasses and woolly gloves; a large die

music no

Place some chocolate buttons on a plate in the centre of the circle, with the clothes nearby. The children sit in a circle and take turns to throw the die (you may need to help them read the numbers). The first to throw a six has to get up, put on the hat, scarf, sunglasses and gloves, and try to pick up a chocolate button. If successful, she can eat it. A variation that adds excitement is for the other children to carry on throwing the die – if a six is thrown before the first child eats their chocolate button, they have to take off all the clothes and let the next child have a go.

Play tip

For older children you can put out a bar of chocolate and a knife and fork, so they have to cut off a piece and eat it with the fork.

changing places

age 4+
props some cushions and some cards with individual numbers written on
music no

Place the cushions in a large circle around the room. Ask all the children, except one, to sit on a cushion. Blindfold this child with a soft scarf and sit him on a cushion in the centre of the circle. Meanwhile give each of the other children a numbered card. Turn the blindfolded child around for a few turns, and then say two numbers out loud. The children holding those two cards have to swap places as quietly as possible to avoid being caught by the blindfolded child. If one of them is caught she has a turn wearing the blindfold in the centre of the circle.

Play tip
Make sure the children cross the circle to get to their new places, rather than creeping around the outside, to give the blindfolded child a fair chance of catching one of them.

make me laugh

age 4+
props none
music no

This is a very silly game that can help to break the ice at parties. One child sits in the centre of the circle. He has to look as serious as possible, and all the other children have to do their utmost to make him laugh. They aren't allowed to touch him (no tickling allowed) but can make any silly face or noise they like. As soon as the central child laughs or even smiles, he is out and another child has a turn. If you want a winner, this will be the child who can keep a straight face the longest.

Play tip
To give everyone a turn more quickly, you can play this game in two rows, with the children facing each other. One row try to keep a straight face, while the row of children facing them try to make them laugh.

'I need the toilet'
Sooner or later you're going to hear these words, and the chances are that you'll be too busy to take the child to the lavatory yourself. So make sure you have an adult assigned to 'toilet duty'.

just ten seconds
age 4+
props a stopwatch, or watch with
a second hand
music no

The children sit in a large circle.
Choose one child to sit in the
centre of the circle and give her
a simple category, such as colours,
animals, shapes or clothes.
Ask her to name as many as
possible in the ten seconds
allowed. Get the other children
to say, 'Ready, Steady, GO!'
together, and time the child as
she lists items from this group.
The child with the most on their
list wins, although it's sensible to
have a small prize for everyone
after this game. If anyone gets
really stuck, let them begin again
with a different category.

Other category ideas include:
- fairytale characters
- types of food
- toys
- musical instruments
- vehicles
- flowers

Play tip
A second adult helper will be
especially useful to make a note
of how many names each child has
come up with, as you'll be busy with
your stopwatch.

CHAPTER 4

lively games

SECRETS OF SUCCESS

Lively games are great fun, but can quickly become chaotic. Here are some tips for keeping things running smoothly:

- Write a list of all the games you're going to play.

- Make sure you have any props to hand.

- Avoid long gaps between games.

- Know the rules inside out – and stick to them.

- Alternate lively games with sitting-down games.

- Have a helper on hand to encourage reluctant players to join in.

limbo dancing

age 6+
props a long, smooth stick
music yes

For this game you'll need lively music, and children who are well into the party spirit. You and another adult hold up the ends of the stick fairly high off the floor. Each child takes a turn to dance in 'limbo' style, bending backwards as they shuffle underneath the stick. Once everyone has gone under the stick, lower it a little, then let them all try again. Anyone who can't get under it or falls over is 'out'. The last child who can get under the lowered stick is declared the winner.

Play tip

Make sure there's a soft surface, like grass or a carpet, in case of bumpy landings.

conga dance

age 3+
props none
music you sing

A great favourite that helps to create a real party feeling. The children form a long line by holding on to each others' waists, with an adult leading them. You dance around the room, singing to the conga tune:

La-la-la-la-la-la-LA!
La-la-la-la-la-la-LA!
La-la-la-la,
La-la-la-la!

At the end of each line, everyone kicks out their right or left leg in time with each other. You can stick to dancing in one room, or weave your way around the house or garden.

Play tip
This can be a fun way to gather together all the children and lead them to the tea table.

Simon says

age 3+
props none
music no

This game is a traditional favourite. The children have to copy your actions each time you say 'Simon says ...', before an instruction. For example, if you say, 'Simon says clap your hands', the children must copy you and clap their hands. If you don't say 'Simon says ...', before an instruction (for example, you say 'Clap your hands'), they must stay still even though you are still doing the action.

Try:
- Running
- Hopping
- Jumping
- Waving your arms in the air
- Doing star jumps
- Creeping with both hands and feet on the floor
- Leaping like a frog
- Putting your hands on your head

Play tip
Alternate boisterous actions with quiet ones, so that the children don't get too exhausted.

find your partner
age 4+
props none
music yes

Stand the children in two circles, the inner one facing the outer one. Ask them to hold hands with the person opposite them and tell them that is their partner, then ask the children to let go of their partner's hands. Put on the music and ask each circle to run around in different directions. When the music stops, they all have to find their partner and sit down. The last couple to sit down is 'out'.

Play tip
If you have an odd number of children, just make one set of three.

pat the balloon
age 3+
props some blown-up balloons
music no

Line the children up and give each one a balloon. When you shout, 'Go!' they all have to pat their balloon across to the other side of the room, keeping them up in the air. If their balloon drops to the floor or they pat someone else's balloon they must go back to the starting line. The first one to get 'home' is the winner.

Play tip
Round balloons are the best shape for this game. Make sure all the children have a balloon of the same size to make it fair.

Staying in control
Make sure any instructions you call out are absolutely clear and leave no room for misinterpretation. Also, make sure all the children can hear what you're saying. It may help to have a practice round before starting a game to ensure everyone knows how to play.

hop, bunny, hop!
age 3+
props none
music no

Ask all the children to hop around the room until you shout, 'Danger – a fox!' when they must stop and stand very still. Anyone who moves is out. When you shout, 'OK, danger's gone,' they can start hopping around again.

Play tip
Vary the source of the danger. Try a hawk, hunter, car, farmer or a cat.

hunt the teddy
age 2+
props a little teddy
music no

Hide the teddy in the sitting-room while the children wait outside. Then let them back in to start searching. If they go near the hiding place call out, 'Getting warmer, getting very warm, getting hot, getting very hot!'; if they move away from the hiding place, call out, 'Getting colder'. Whoever finds the teddy gets to hide it for the next round.

Play tip
If you haven't got a small teddy, use any small object (nothing sharp or so small that they might swallow it) – but, if it's unusual, show the children what they are looking for first.

traffic lights

age 2+
props circles of red, orange and green card (optional)
music no

All the children run around the room pretending to be cars, bikes or lorries. When you shout out, 'RED LIGHT!' they all have to stop and keep absolutely still. Then you call, 'GREEN LIGHT!' and they can start moving again. When you say, 'ORANGE LIGHT!' they have to slow right down to a walking pace. No one wins – but everyone has fun. To finish the game, direct all the children to 'park' in a line.

Play tip
Very young children may find it easier to respond if you hold up an appropriate coloured circle at the same time as calling out the traffic light colour.

picture treasure hunt

age 3+
props clear picture clues of safe and easy-to-find places in the house
music no

Prepare a set of picture clues and lay them in a trail around the house and garden before the party. For example, the clues could be pictures of the television, the sofa, a bed, the bath, a large toy, a table, the swing, the sandpit or a flowerpot. Show the children the first clue, ask them what it is, then set off with them to find it. You'll need to go with them to help those who need it and make sure one child doesn't rush ahead. The 'treasure' needs to include a small prize for each child (such as a little farm animal or bouncy ball) – you could hide them on the spot or award them when each spot is found.

Play tip
This game works best with a small group of children, otherwise there are too many children hunting the same clue.

post-box race

age 5+

props three 'post-boxes' (shoeboxes will do) with three different animal pictures stuck on each (nine animals in all) and twenty-seven small animal cards (three cards showing each of the same nine animals). You can vary the numbers of cards according to numbers of children.

music no

Put each post-box in a different room and show the children where they are. Then give the children one animal card each, writing their name or initials on the back, and send them off to post their cards in the matching post-box. When a child has posted his first card, he races back to you for another, and off he goes again. When all the cards have been used up, count up how many each child has posted correctly to find the winner. Don't forget to put the names on the backs of the cards!

Play tip
Your child may enjoy helping you prepare the post-boxes and cards for this game.

pass the balloon

age 4+

props some sausage-shaped balloons

music no

Line the children up in two rows, well spaced apart. Give the two children at the start of each row a balloon to hold between their knees. When you say, 'Go!' they have to waddle up to the next person in their line and pass the balloon to them, without using their hands. That person then turns around and waddles to the next child with the balloon between their knees. If anyone drops the balloon, they go back to their own starting position. The last child has to waddle back to the starting position. The first team to get their balloon to the starting position without dropping it is the winner.

Play tip
For older children, you could carry on this game until the original team leader is back at the front of the line.

Stay safe
Pick up any bits of popped balloons immediately, as they can be a choking hazard for younger children.

throw the tissue

age 3+
props scrunched up tissue paper
or pieces of kitchen roll
music no

Simply ask the children to take
turns to throw a ball of
scrunched up paper and measure
whose ball goes farthest.

Play tip
You could play this in rows of three
or four children at a time and have a
play-off with the winners.

twisties

age 5+
props none
music no

One child stands with her back to
the others, who hold hands in a
circle. They get themselves all
tangled up by climbing over each
others' legs and crossing arms.
Then the other child turns round
and has to try to untangle the
others.

Play tip
Make sure the tangled children stay
holding hands the entire time, or the
untangler won't have a chance.

make-believe animals

age 2+
props none
music yes

Start the game by saying, 'When the music begins, I want you to hop around the room like rabbits.' When the music stops, the children have to freeze until you tell them the next animal to be, and the music starts again. For the final round, the children have to, 'ROAR like a lion!'.

Suggestions to try:
• Slither like a snake
• Leap like a frog
• Swim like a fish
• Flap like a bird
• Prowl like a cat
• Trot like a pony
• Scamper like a mouse

Play tip
To help the children along a little, show them the action as you name each animal.

find the island

age 2+
props one cushion for each child
music yes

Scatter the cushions randomly around the room. Then tell the children to swim in the 'sea' (the carpet) as the music plays, but when the music stops, you call out, 'Help, there's a storm coming! Get to the islands!' The children then have to find a cushion to sit on so that they're not touching the floor. Anyone with any part of his body touching the floor is out. Vary the danger by saying 'pirates', 'sharks', 'a whirlwind', 'crocodiles', and so on.

Play tip
To find a winner, remove one cushion with each round until only one child is left in the game.

jelly shapes
age 3+
props cardboard circle, square, rectangle and triangle
music optional

This game works best with a group of at least eight children. The children stand up and pretend to be wobbly jelly blobs, until you tell them that in a moment all the jelly blobs are going to be poured into a big bowl and made into one large shape. Tell the children the shape is a ROUND jelly (hold up the cardboard circle to be sure they know the shape) – they must join hands and try to make a big circle. Then say, 'Oh no! The jelly's melting!' and the children must go back to being individual wobbly blobs again. Continue the game with different shaped jellies – each time the children hold hands to form the outline of the shape.

Video know-how
If you put on a video at the end of the party while you wait for parents, choose one that features short episodes rather than a feature film, so there's a natural end to each story, allowing children to leave.

Play tip
At the end of the game, you could give all the children a jelly sweet.

all line up!

age 5+
props none
music no

This is a co-operative game, as the children work together within their teams – you may need to step in and help out younger children.

First divide the children into two teams, each with an adult helper. Then ask the children to line themselves up in order of height, starting with the smallest and building up to the tallest. The first team to do this wins a point. The next challenge is for the teams to form a different line-up according to their hair length. Again, the first team to finish wins a point. The final challenge is for the teams to regroup themselves according to alphabetical order of their first names. (They will probably need quite a bit of help with this.) The team with the most points after three rounds is the winner.

Play tip
If you prefer to keep the game non-competitive, it's just as easy to play with all the children at once and give each child a small prize at the end for joining in.

flap the fish

age 2+
props paper fish and some newspapers
music no

Before the party, cut out some large fish from paper. At the party, lay the fish in a row and give each child a folded newspaper to flap up and down to make their fish 'swim' across to the other side of the room. The one who gets there first is the winner.

Play tip
If you have too many children to play this altogether, let some sit out and colour in their fish before it's their turn.

how long can you hop?
age 3+
props none
music yes

In this game the idea is to challenge the children to do a particular movement for a certain length of time. Ask them to start hopping on one leg while you play the music. If they stop or put down their other leg they must sit down on the spot. The last one left hopping is the winner. You could also try some other challenges, such as skipping or star jumps. Always follow this game with a sitting down game and a drink, as it can be very tiring for children.

Play tip
If the children are too young to hop, get them to jump instead, but be prepared for the game to last longer.

magic mirrors
age 4+
props none
music optional

Divide the children into pairs and get them to face each other. Call the first member of each pair a 'mirror' and the second a 'reflection'. Ask all the mirrors to mime an action, such as pretending to eat a meal or brushing their teeth, and then ask all the reflections to copy the mirrors' movements. Mirrors can move their hands, heads, arms and upper body, but not their legs or feet (this is to prevent the children knocking into each other). After a few minutes swap mirrors and reflections around so that everyone has a turn to lead.

Play tip
You may want to play some music so the children can have a go at copying each others' dancing movements. Have a selection of different types of music to inspire your mirrors to move in different ways.

balls in the bucket

age 4+

props two large buckets and lots of small soft balls

music no

This is really an outside game, although you can play it indoors with very young children. Put the buckets at one end of the garden, mark a 'line', where the children stand to throw the balls, then divide the children into two teams. Give each child at least one ball. When you say 'Go', the first child in each team runs towards the line, stops, and tries to throw her ball into her team's bucket. Whether or not she gets it in, she runs back to her team, touches the next person's hand as a signal for them to go, and joins the end the queue. The game finishes when all the children have had their turn and the team with the most balls in its bucket wins. You can extend the game by letting the teams play two or three rounds.

Play tip

Younger children don't need to race in teams, they'll simply enjoy trying to throw their balls in a bucket.

Keeping things fair

Often with lively games one child emerges as a frequent winner. If this is the case, try to engineer the game so that other children get a chance, or so that the whole team wins a prize.

CHAPTER 5

quiet games

SECRETS OF SUCCESS

Quiet games are essential to balance any party. Play one when the children are getting too boisterous, too hot or straight after tea.

- For games with props, make sure you have everything you need before the party.

- Plan to have a good mix of games with and without props, so there isn't too much preparation needed.

- Keep craft-based games towards the end of the party, as these need time for tidying away and cleaning up.

- Save a couple of quiet games that don't need props for sticky moments when you want to change the mood quickly.

- Even quiet games need adult helpers, so make sure there's at least one other grown-up assisting you.

sleepy lions

age 3+
props none
music no

An excellent way to cool down even the liveliest and most competitive child. All of the guests have to lie down on the floor and pretend to be lions who are very tired and have fallen fast asleep. Tell the children that the lions are not able to move at all, and if anyone so much as twitches they'll have to wake up and be out of the game. Any children who are out can try to make the others move, but without touching them.

Play tip

Keep your voice low and murmur the instructions to help the children relax. Ignore any movement for a few minutes to give all the children a chance to wind down.

Welcome

Tie some balloons to the front door or gate to welcome the guests. This is also a great way for parents who haven't visited you before to identify the party venue.

pin the tail on the piggy

age 4+

props a large picture of a pig with no tail, a 'tail' for each child with his name written on it, a soft scarf for a blindfold

music no

Stick up the picture of the pig at a height that the children can reach easily, and mark the spot where the tail should be. Sit the children on the floor. Call up one child, cover his eyes gently with the blindfold, and turn him around. Then give him a tail with his name on it and lead him to the picture. Ask him to stick the tail where he thinks it should go on the picture. You then remove the blindfold and the next child has a turn. The winner is the child who has stuck a tail nearest to the right spot.

Play tip

Make curly tails for a pig by drawing spirals and cutting along the line towards the middle. Drawing pins are normally used to stick the tail on but it's safer for young children to use sticky tape.

what's missing?

age 3+

props a large tray with a selection of small objects on it

music no

Ask the children to have a good look at all the things on the tray and remember as many as they can. Then ask them to close their eyes tightly (or take the tray out of the room) and remove a single item. Then ask them to open their eyes again, and see if they can guess what's missing. Then play again, removing an item each time until there's only one left.

Play tip

For older children, you can play the traditional version of this game – when you cover the tray or take it away, each child writes down as many items as they can remember.

what animal are you?

age 2+
props none
music no

The children all sit in a circle. You call one child forward and whisper an animal to them. They then act out that animal (without making any noises) to the others, who have to guess what animal it could be. The one who gets it right acts out the next animal.

Play tip
For really little children, allow them to make the appropriate noise to help the others guess.

bunny in the burrow

age 3+
props a large cloth or blanket
music no

The children all lie on the floor, with plenty of room between them. Ask them to close their eyes very tightly, as the bunnies are all in their burrows under the ground. Carefully put the cloth over one of the children, then tell the others it's time to wake up and open their eyes. The child under the blanket stays still while the others gather round and try to guess who is missing.

Play tip
Before you begin, show the children how you'll be covering one of them with a blanket, so no one gets scared. Play the game often enough for everyone to have a turn at being the bunny.

what's in the box?

age 3+
props two boxes with holes cut in the sides and six objects to put in each box, all of which are easily identifiable by touch
music no

Before the party, place the objects securely in the boxes. Divide the children into two teams, each with an adult. Ask the first child in each team to put their hand inside, feel an item and say (or write down) what she thinks it is. Once she has named an item, the next child in the team has a go. The first team to name all six items correctly is the winner.

Suggestions for feely items:
- An orange
- A sock
- A hairbrush
- A wooden spoon
- A ball
- A comb
- A toothbrush
- An Alice band
- A dry sponge

Play tip
If you haven't got cardboard boxes, use pillowcases instead.

mask parade

age 4+
props one paper plate with eyeholes cut out and a piece of elastic attached around the back for each child, colouring pens and a selection of stick-on items like plastic jewels, sequins, wool or feathers.
music no

This works best with small party groups – especially girls – as you'll need to supervise closely. Sit the children around a table (or on the floor with a sheet of newspaper) and give each one a mask to decorate. When they have all finished have a parade around the room.

Play tip
Use only glue sticks rather than runny glue in a pot, as this is bound to tip over and spill.

fishing pool

age 2+
props a large sheet or tablecloth, a 'rod' (a stick with a piece of string tied to it), and some small, lightweight, wrapped presents
music no

Hang the sheet or tablecloth at waist height across one part of the room (use a string tied across two kitchen chairs) so that the children cannot see behind it. Then sit the children on one side and call one child up to go fishing. Give him the rod and let him fish over the top of the sheet for a present. You'll need an adult behind the sheet to tie the present on to the string.

Play tip
Make sure all the presents are ones that would appeal to everyone, such as crayons or stickers.

Knock, knock
Make sure the door is never opened by a child during the party, and don't leave the door open at any time as a child, especially a younger brother or sister, could wander out.

fluttering butterflies

age 2+
props none
music no

This is a first nature game that holds their concentration and helps quieten them down. The children start off by curling up in a tiny ball pretending to be a butterfly egg. Next they hatch out and stretch in the sun. Then they become proper caterpillars, crawling around and munching leaves. Next, they have to weave themselves a cocoon by waving their arms all around themselves and then lying still. Finally they hatch out into beautiful butterflies and flutter around the room.

Play tip
To add a bit of excitement, occasionally call out 'Look out, a blackbird's overhead!', so all the caterpillars have to keep very still and hide.

20 questions

age 5+
props none
music no

Whisper the name of an object (say a tiger, a daffodil or a train) to one child and give the other children a clue as to what sort of object it is – say, an animal, a plant or a vehicle. The children then have to ask the first child questions to try to guess what the object is. If they guess correctly within 20 questions, they've won the game.

Play tip
Older children can begin the game by asking the question, 'Animal, vegetable or mineral?' but younger ones will probably find this a bit too complicated.

wobbly sweets

age 3+
props a bag of small sweets
music no

All the children lie on their backs, on the floor. Go around and place a small sweet on each child's forehead. When every child has a sweet, ask them to do things that might make the sweet fall off. If the sweet does fall off, the child can eat it but is then out of the game. The last child with the sweet still on his forehead is the winner.

Tricks to ask them to try :
• Raising their feet in the air
• Shaking their arms
• Touching their noses
• Sticking their tongues out
• Bending their knees up and down
• Singing *Baa Baa Black Sheep*

Play tip
It's best to choose wrapped sweets for this game so they don't get dirty when they fall to the floor.

hide and seek pairs

age 3+
props two packs of playing cards
music no

Hide all the cards from one pack around the room. Deal the second pack evenly between the children, then set them off to find the cards that match the ones in their hand. The first child to find all of their matching pairs stands still. The others line up behind her as they find all theirs.

Play tip
Use fewer cards for younger children if a whole pack is too daunting.

quick draw

age 5+
props a roll of plain lining paper and plenty of felt-tip pens and colouring pencils
music no

Have some pieces of paper cut to roughly the same length as the height of the children. Divide the children up into groups of two or three and, ideally, put each team in a different room. Let them choose one person in the group to draw around (you may need to help), then colour in the features and clothes. When everyone has finished, get each team to hold up their figure and see if the others can guess who it is.

Play tip
Measure your own child and add a bit extra to get the right size for the pieces of paper.

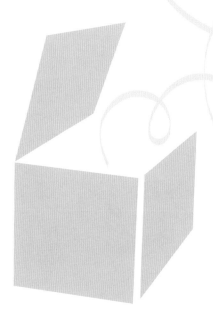

lucky quiz

age 3+

props a box filled with little wrapped presents, ideally hidden among polystyrene pieces or scrunched up tissue paper

music no

The children sit around the prize box and you ask the group a question. They put their hands up if they know the answer. You choose a child, and if they're right, they can pick a lucky dip prize from the box.

Play tip

For very young children, ask each child an easy individual question, such as, 'What sound does a duck make?' so that they have a chance to win.

Party boxes

If you want to cut down on the clearing up, you could pack the children's party teas in individual cardboard boxes so they can go straight in the bin afterwards. They're expensive, but children love them and they also give you the option of being able to transport tea outside easily if the weather's fine.

crazy raisins

age 5+

props chopsticks, a piece of paper, a bowl and a mini box of raisins for each child

music no

Lay 20 raisins for each child out on a sheet of paper and give him a bowl and a set of chopsticks. On the command, 'Go!', all the children pick up the raisins one by one with their chopsticks and transfer them to the bowl without dropping them. Any that are dropped are left where they are, and the child continues with those that are left. The one with the most raisins in their bowl at the end is the winner.

Play tip

If you don't have chopsticks, get the children to suck up the raisins on the end of a straw to move them instead.

we're behind you!
age 4+
props a soft scarf
music yes

One child is blindfolded and has their hand held by a helper. The others all wander round the room until told to 'Stop'. Point to several of them. They have to creep as quietly as possible to stand behind the blindfolded child. After they have lined up, ask the blindfolded child to guess how many children are standing behind him. If he gets it right, everyone claps; if he gets it wrong, say 'A few more ...' or 'A few less ...' to give him a chance to find the right answer.

Play tip
The reward for guessing the correct number is to choose the next child to be blindfolded.

guess the number
age 5+
props several clear sealed pots or jars filled with items such as chocolate beans, dried pasta shells, strips of ribbon or clothes pegs.
music no

Before the party, prepare the jars of objects and make a note of how many are in each one. At the party, sit the children down and put one jar on the floor in front of them so they all can see it. Then ask them to guess how many items they think are in that jar. Each child says their guess out loud, and the one closest to the correct number wins a small prize. Do the same for each jar.

Play tip
This game can also be played with younger children, but stick to larger objects and limit the number of items in each jar to below ten.

what's different?

age 4+
props a few toys, cushions or other colourful items
music no

This is an observation game that will encourage the children to settle down quietly and look hard at their surroundings. Explain that something is going to be changed or moved in a room and that they have to see if they can spot the difference. You may want to restrict this to an area of a room, especially if the children aren't familiar with your house. Ask the children to look around carefully, noticing all the cushions, ornaments and so on. Then get one of them to go out of the room for a minute while something is changed – perhaps moving a teddy from one chair to another when he wasn't there before, or removing a brightly coloured cushion. Then invite the child back in and see how quickly he can spot what has changed.

Play tip
Another version of this game is to send one child out while you add something to another child's outfit, for example a ribbon in a girl's hair or a brooch on her dress, or a card tucked down inside a boy's sock.

animal parade
age 4+
props none
music no

This fun memory game will encourage your guests to sit and concentrate, and so may work best with a small group of children. Sit the children in a circle. Start the game by saying, 'One dog'. Each child has to repeat this until it comes back to you. The child next to you then adds another animal, saying, 'One dog, two cats', and this travels around the group until it comes back to that child. The person sitting next to her then adds a new animal, saying, 'One dog, two cats, three mice', and the game continues until someone forgets what's on the list. That person is then 'out' and the others continue until one child is left as the winner.

Play tip
Choose other categories according to the interests of the children at your party, such as sport or flowers.

funny face balloons
age 3+
props round party balloons and broad-tipped felt pens
music no

Give each child a balloon and a felt pen and ask them to draw a funny face on their balloon.

Play tip
Play this as a type of 'consequences' by asking one child to do the eyes, then pass on their balloon for the next child to draw the nose, and so on, with mouths, ears and hair.

Back to basics
Stock up on plenty of loo rolls, kitchen rolls and wipes so that you're prepared for the inevitable spills and clean-ups.

funny pictures

age 5+
props pencils, paper and some colouring pens
music optional

Give each child a piece of paper and a pencil, and allow them one minute to draw the head and neck of a funny person before folding the paper over to hide the picture. (They may need help with this, as it's best to leave a little bit of the neck showing to guide the next player.) Everyone then passes the paper to the person on their left, who then draws a body and arms, and folds the paper again. Next come the legs, and finally the shoes. The papers are passed round one more time and then unfolded and shown to everyone else for a good laugh. The finished pictures can be coloured in if the children want to.

Play tip
Older children can also add a funny name to their character if they want.

CHAPTER 6

chasing games

SECRETS OF SUCCESS

C atching or chasing games give children an opportunity to run around and use up some energy. However, make sure you remain firmly in control.

- Explain how important it is to stick to the rules in these sorts of games.

- Always check that you've got all the equipment you need.

- If your chasing game is a hectic one, make sure you do it before the party tea.

- It's best to do catching games outside, so the children have plenty of room.

- For ball games with younger children, use a big, soft ball that's easy to catch.

- If younger children are finding it hard to catch the ball, move them closer toward it. Move older children farther apart.

what's the time, Mr Wolf?

age 5+
props none
music no

Choose one child to be Mr Wolf (or be him yourself to start with). He stands at one end of the garden, facing away from the other children. Line the others up at the opposite end of the garden. When you say, 'Go!' the children take one step forwards, shouting out, 'What's the time, Mr Wolf?' Mr Wolf may answer any time from one o'clock to twelve o'clock, in which case the children can take another step forward. But if Mr Wolf says, 'Dinner time!' he turns and chases the children back to the starting line. If he catches one, that child becomes Mr Wolf.

Play tip

If you're playing in a big space outside, the children can take the same number of steps as the time Mr Wolf says, for example, six steps when Mr Wolf says, 'Six o'clock.'

Grandmother's footsteps

age 5+
props none
music no

One child is chosen to be Grandmother. She stands at one end of the room with her back turned to the other children, who all line up at the other end of the room. When you say 'Go', they have to creep up on the Grandmother as quietly as possible. Grandmother can turn around suddenly as often as she likes, and the other players have to stand still. If she sees anyone move or wobble, they have to go back to the beginning. The first one to reach Grandmother without being detected has the next turn at being Grandmother.

Play tip
You'll need to 'help' Grandmother to decide who has moved or not when she turns round, as this can be hotly disputed by the child who's being sent back to the start again!

frogs and fairies

age 2+
props none
music optional

This simple game is lovely for very young children. Tell the children they are all giants, and when you say, 'Go!' they have to dance around the room using giant steps and actions. When you say, 'Stop!' they have to rush to catch a partner, then freeze holding hands. You then give them a new character to be, for example fairies, frogs, bunnies, spacemen or robots. When you say, 'Go!' again, they let go of their partner and dance in the new way, for example hopping like frogs.

Play tip
If there's an uneven number of children you can step in to be a child's partner. Tell the children they must choose a different partner each time.

giant steps, pigeon steps

age 3+
props none
music optional

Stand at one end of the room, with the children lined up facing you. Show them a selection of steps. For example, Giant Step means a big stride, Pigeon Step means putting one foot carefully in front of the other, Side Step means shuffling sideways and Tip-toe Step means what it says. You then give instructions so the children move towards you, saying, 'One giant step ... five pigeon steps ... three tip-toe steps ...', for example, until the first child reaches you. They then become the next to have a turn at giving the instructions.

Play tip
For older children, add additional instructions such as 'Freeze!' when they must stand still, or 'Back to base!' when they all have to run as fast as they can back to the starting line.

step-toes

age 3+
props sheets of paper or newspaper
music no

Give each child two sheets of paper. He has to work his way across the room by placing one piece of paper in front of himself at a time, and stepping on it. He can only move forward by moving the papers – he's not allowed to step on the floor. The first child to get across the room is the winner.

Play tip
Older children can play this in teams like a relay race.

stuck in the mud
age 5+
props none
music no

This game is fast and furious, and best played outside. Choose one child to be 'It'. He chases all the others and if he touches anyone they immediately become 'stuck in the mud'. This means they must stand still with their legs apart. Any other child who is still free can crawl through their legs, which then sets them free from the mud to run around again. If the child is caught while trying to free someone else, they too are then stuck in the mud. The last person to be caught has the next go at being 'It'.

Play tip
If there are lots of children playing, any child caught while trying to free another could join the first child in being 'It'.

hot potato
age 5+
props a ball
music no

The children stand in a circle with a reasonable space between each one. Give one child a ball – the 'hot potato' – and ask them to name another child quickly before throwing the ball to them. If the named child catches it, he immediately chooses someone else to throw the ball to. If he misses it, he is out of the game. The last catcher remaining is the winner.

Play tip
You could roll the ball between seated children if they are too young to catch.

Place names
If you have a mix of boys and girls at the party, they're likely to split quickly into gender groups. Help them to mix – and to keep the atmosphere calmer – by putting a mini name plate at each place at the table. Your child may enjoy helping you to make these.

40, 40, home
age 5+
props none
music no

Choose a base camp (for example a tree or bush). One child is chosen to be 'It'. That person closes their eyes and slowly counts to 20, giving the others time to hide. 'It' comes looking for them, and they have to try to get back to the base camp without being caught. If they make it back, they shout, '40, 40 Home!' But if they're caught on the way, they're 'out'.

Play tip
Make sure that the base camp is fairly sturdy, as running children will probably crash into it with some vigour!

Teatime tricks
When you're planning the party tea put out the savoury food first, holding back the sweet treats until the children have eaten at least some reasonably nutritious and filling foods, like mini sandwiches, pizza slices or little sausages.

ping pong catch
age 5+
props two ping pong balls and a box of plastic straws
music no

Divide the children into two teams. Choose one child from each team to stand at the far end of the room, facing his team. Give each child a straw; and the first child in each team a ping pong ball as well. When you say, 'Go!' that child has to blow the ping pong ball towards their team-mate at the other end of the room. As soon as he can, the waiting child catches the ball and runs back with it, handing it to the next person in the line, who blows the ball towards the new person at the end. The first team in which everyone has had a go is the winner.

Play tip
You will need a line at the far end of the room to stop the child who is catching the ball going too far towards the person blowing the ping pong ball.

knees down, knees up

age 5+
props a soft ball
music no

Stand the children around the room in a loose circle. Name a child and throw the ball to him. If he catches it successfully, he names another child and throws the ball on to him. If a child misses a catch, he has to kneel down on one knee. The next time he misses, he goes down on two knees. The third time he misses, he has to put one hand behind his back. If you're playing on a soft surface, the next forfeit can be to lie down. A final miss and the child is out.

Play tip
If the child manages to catch a ball, you can reverse the forfeit one step at a time, so that if a child is on two knees when he catches the ball he then moves back onto one knee.

round the clock catching

age 5+
props a soft ball
music no

Each child takes a turn to bounce the ball once. If everyone manages this successfully, they all try to bounce it twice, then three times and so on. Anyone who misses a bounce is out. The child who can bounce it the most times is the winner. You can try this as a catching game too, with each child having to throw the ball in the air and catch it once, then twice and so on.

Play tip
Stick to small groups for this game or it takes too long for the turns to come around.

Noah's ark

age 3+
props animal names written on folded cards (make two cards for each animal)
music no

Fold the cards in half then mix them up in a hat. Let each child pick out one card. They discover what their animal is, but have to keep it secret. When you say, 'Go!' they have to travel around the room making the right animals noises and movements. As they do so they have to find their animal partner and stand beside them, making their noises until everyone is paired up. Then mix the cards back up in the hat, and play again. If there is an odd number of children, make one animal a group of three.

Play tip
If the children are too young to read the cards, draw simple pictures of the animals instead.

chicken chase

age 4+
props none
music no

One child stands at one end of the room or garden to be the first chicken. Another child is chosen to be the fox and stands in the centre of the room, while the rest of the children stand together at the other end. The first chicken calls another child by name, and that chicken has to try to get across the room to join the first chicken without being caught by the fox. If the fox catches her she has to sit or stand still on the spot, and another chicken is chosen to run across. The last child to get across without being caught is the next fox.

Play tip
This game is best played outside, since you need a fair amount of space for it.

crocodile river

age 3+
props two skipping ropes
music no

Lie the skipping ropes a couple of metres apart to make a 'crocodile river'. Then ask all the children to run around the room until you shout 'Stop!'. Anyone in the river when you shout, 'Stop!' is eaten by crocodiles and is 'out'.

Play tip
The children may feel it's fairer if you have your back turned toward them when you shout, 'Stop!'

egg-and-spoon race

age 4+
props several hard-boiled eggs and some dessert spoons
music no

Either line all the children up or divide them into two teams to play this as a relay race. Each child has to run from the starting line to the finishing line, balancing their egg in their spoon. If it drops, they have to go back to the start again.

Play tip
If you don't want to use eggs, you could use small uncooked potatoes in their place.

Late leavers
Have some basic craft activities (like felt-tip pens and paper) handy for quiet activities at the end of the party, when you're waiting for the last few parents to arrive.

wheelbarrow race
age 5+
props none
music no

This is a traditional race that most people will remember from their own childhood. Pair up the children and ask one to be the 'wheelbarrow' and the other to be the 'gardener'. The gardeners then hold the wheelbarrows' ankles while the wheelbarrows walk along on their hands. They line up, and, on the command 'GO!' race off to the finishing line as quickly as possible.

Play tip
Keep the race track short as the children will get tired very quickly – and make sure everyone gets a go at being the wheelbarrow.

mix-up relay
age 3+
props none
music optional

This is best played outside as clear start/finish and return lines need to be marked out – and the children will get very excited. Divide the children into two teams. The first member of each team has to run to the return line and put his foot on it, but must then turn round and walk back. Any player who tries to run must go back to the return line (you'll need an adult there to check that no-one is cheating). As soon as he gets back, the second member of the team sets off at a run, and so on until all the team have each run to the return line and walked back. The first team to finish are the winners.

Play tip
For older children you could add harder movements, such as hopping down to the line and skipping back.

Standing on ceremony
Make every child feel special at the end of the party by giving them all a home-made medal. Make these from loops of gold ribbon decorated with stickers and sequins.

hold your ankles

age 4+
props none
music no

This is a simple racing game, but with a twist. Divide the children into two teams, each lining up behind a leader. Then each child has to run in turn to a line at the opposite end of the garden and back holding onto their ankles. It sounds simple, but in fact is quite difficult – and very silly!

Play tip
This game can be made easier by setting another challenge, such as getting the children to run with their hands on their knees or clasped on top of their heads.

tag

age 5+
props none
music no

Choose one child to be 'It'. She chases the others, and anyone she touches immediately becomes another catcher too. It doesn't take long before everyone's been caught! The last survivor then becomes 'It' for the next game.

Play tip
You can try letting one child remain 'It' throughout the game, but she is likely to get very tired chasing the rest of the children on her own.

pony jumping

age 4+
props flowerpots, bamboo sticks
music no

Set up a simple 'show-jumping course' by propping bamboo sticks across upturned flowerpots. Vary the height by stacking the flowerpots on top of each other, and put some jumps close together to make the course more challenging. The children have to pretend to be ponies, and take turns to jump the course. Ask each child to choose their own pony name before they set off on the course.

Play tip
Give each child a gold star to stick on their top when they have finished, even if they didn't get a clear round.

follow my leader

age 2+
props none
music no

This is not exactly a chasing game, but it is an outdoor game that even very young children can enjoy. Divide the children into two lines, with an adult leader at the front. On the word 'GO!' each leader sets off towards the finishing line weaving around and doing funny actions as they go, such as waving their arms, wiggling their fingers in the air, flapping their elbows or crouching down low. The children behind follow their movements until they cross the finishing line.

Play tip
There's no rush with this game, but the adult helpers should make sure that the two teams tie as they cross the finishing line.

swap the sweets

age 3+
props two plates, two bowls, and
two wrapped sweets for each child
music optional

This is a simple relay race. Divide
the children into two teams. Each
team has a plate of sweets at one
end of the room and an empty
bowl at the start/finish line. At
the command 'GO!' the first
member of each team has to run
to the other end of the room,
collect a sweet, then bring it back
to be put in his team's bowl. The
next player runs down to collect
their sweet, and so on. Each
player should run twice, until all
the sweets have been collected.
The first team to collect them all
is the winner, but the real prize is
that each player gets to eat their
two sweets!

Play tip
If you think the children might eat
the sweets before the end, or you'd
prefer them not to eat sweets at all,
you could play this with buttons or
other small items.

parties for all ages

This chapter contains an at-a-glance selection of games for each age group, with tips and ideas for themes, going-home presents and special activities, and references to a selection of suitable games listed in the main part of the book.

the **1st** birthday

Your baby's first birthday is a moment which deserves real celebration. From being a helpless newborn he's now an active, giggling, cuddly little person.

the **2nd** birthday

Although your two-year-old won't yet be able to anticipate the excitement of a birthday party, she'll really enjoy all the fun and games once the other children have arrived and the party has begun.

the **3rd** birthday

By the age of three, your child will probably have a small group of children she regularly plays with.

the **5th** birthday and beyond

You'll be well into the swing of parties by the time your child is five. From this age you may want to invite larger numbers – or even the whole class – and it's now that you may want to think about hiring an entertainer.

the **4th** birthday

Birthday parties are a key event for your four-year-old. She may already have been to several and will be anticipating her own with great excitement.

the **1**st birthday

Your baby's first birthday is a moment which deserves real celebration. From being a helpless newborn he's now an active, giggling, cuddly little person. You'll want his party to go with a swing but, to avoid tears, think about the following:

- Limit the number of guests, so your baby doesn't feel overwhelmed by strangers.

- Consider having the party in the morning or at lunchtime to avoid afternoon naps.

- Set out popular baby toys, such as plastic tea sets, pull-along toys and shape-sorters.

- Have some quiet activities for older siblings. Try crayons and colouring books, or mini pots of modelling clay.

- Have a quiet room for babies who want a nap, or who need feeding or changing.

- Offer some grown-up food and drink for the parents.

baby games

Obviously babies aren't ready to join in older children's games, so you won't find party game suggestions from other chapters here. However, they will still enjoy the activities below.

say hello
Parents sit in a circle with their babies on their laps and sing:

Say hello, hello.
Say hello, hello.
Say hello (baby's name).
(A new baby is introduced at the end of each verse.)

roll the ball
with all the babies sitting in a circle, roll a large soft ball across the centre from one to another.

ring-a-ring o'roses

With all of the parents holding their babies, walk around in a circle singing the following rhyme together:

> *Ring-a-ring o' roses,*
> *A pocket full of posies.*
> *A-tishoo! A-tishoo!*
> *We all fall down.*
>
> *The cows are in the meadow*
> *Eating all the grass.*
> *A-tishoo! A-tishoo!*
> *Who's up last!*

When it gets to 'all fall down', everyone bends their knees and bounces down slightly.

tickle my tummy

Slowly recite *Round and Round the Garden* all together, then tickle the babies' tummies to make them giggle:

> *Round and round the garden*
> *Like a teddy bear.*
> *One step, two step*
> *Tickly under there!*

peek-a-boo

This all-time favourite is more fun if lots of babies are doing it at the same time. Try building up to the 'Peek-a-boo!' by counting up to three first.

outdoor fun

If you're lucky enough to have both a garden and a baby with a summer birthday, lay on some outdoor activities, such as a paddling pool, water toys, low rocking toys, dolls' prams, or even a baby slide. *Make sure there's always an adult around to supervise this sort of play.*

going home presents

You don't really need to provide party bags for babies, but if you want to you could include a slice of birthday cake, a piece of gingerbread cut into the shape of the child's initial, a rubber toy animal, some egg-shaped crayons (easy for little hands to grip) or some first construction bricks. Don't put in sticky sweets, balloons, streamers or anything that has small parts, as these could be dangerous for a baby.

happy birthday

This key song can be sung as a game rather than at teatime, when the babies (and parents) may be preoccupied with eating. Everyone sits in a circle around the birthday baby, who is safe on his parent's lap, and serenades him.

pat the toy

Each parent and baby has a soft toy which they stroke while the music plays. When the music stops, they all pat, kiss or hug their toy.

dance with me

Each parent holds their baby and sings: 'This is the way we dance about...' to the tune of Here We Go Round The Mulberry Bush, only with the last line changed to: 'All at a birthday party'. Try different movements, such as jumping, wiggling, skipping, or stamping.

This is the way we dance about,
Dance about, dance about.
This is the way we dance about,
All at a birthday party.

find your nose

Name different parts of the body, such as nose, mouth, eyes, ears, feet and tummy, and get the babies to point to them.

knock down the tower

Each parent builds a small pile of bricks into a tower. When you say, 'Ready, steady, down it comes!' the babies knock the towers down.

Other great games for your one-year-old are:
- Row the boat (see page 22)
- If you're happy and you know it (see page 23)
- The wheels on the bus (see page 27)

the **2**nd birthday

Although your two-year-old won't yet be able to anticipate the excitement of a birthday party, she'll really enjoy all the fun and games once the other children have arrived and the party has begun. Here are some things to consider:

- Your child is still too young to have formed friendships, but will enjoy the company of other children. Make sure you include some children who are familiar to your toddler.

- Parents will need to stay with their children throughout the party. This means you'll need to think about numbers carefully.

- Remember you'll still need a place for nappy changing, as well as somewhere any baby can go to sleep if he suddenly gets tired.

- As with first birthdays, mornings are often a good time for toddler parties, as older siblings are often busy at nursery or school.

toddler games

Two-year-olds are still too little to play many organized games like the ones in this book, but here are some other fun ideas for you to try.

Humpty Dumpty
The toddlers sit on their parents' laps and bounce as everyone sings *Humpty Dumpty*:

*Humpty Dumpty sat on a wall.
Humpty Dumpty had a big fall.
All the king's horses and all the king's men,
couldn't put Humpty together again.*

At the words '*...had a great fall*', all the parents dip their babies between their legs, then lift them up again for the words '*...together again!*'

run to me

Stand the children at one end of the room and the mums at the other. When you say, 'Ready, steady, go!' the toddlers run to their mums or dads for a hug.

incy wincy spider

The children all sit opposite their parents and try to copy the hand and finger actions as everyone sings the song.

Incy Wincy spider,
climbing up the spout.
Down came the rain and
washed poor Incy out!
Out came the sunshine,
and dried up all the rain.
So Incy Wincy spider
climbed up the spout again!

Jack in the box

Ask the children to crouch down on the floor. You hum a laa-laa tune to build up the excitement and then suddenly say, 'Jack in the box!' – at which point all the children have to jump up.

story circle

The children sit in a circle on their parents' laps while you tell or read a familiar story.

Good choices include:
- Goldilocks and the Three Bears
- The Three Little Pigs
- The Little Red Hen

The right time

Toddlers can quickly get tired and cross. Rather than the more usual two hours, you may want to limit the party to one and a half hours. This still gives you plenty of time for free play, a few organized games and a birthday meal. Parents of very young children will almost certainly appreciate you organizing a normal meal for toddlers instead of sticky sweet foods.

from baby to toddler

By the age of two, your child can understand most of what you say, and may be beginning to talk herself. Although most toddlers enjoy playing alongside other children, they aren't yet able to play actively with another child. This is a normal developmental stage, but it does mean that they'll probably be happiest playing with toys individually and will need lots of adult supervision.

farmyard walk

You start a story by saying, 'One day I went to a farm and when I was there I saw some ducks. What sound do ducks make?' The children all make quacking sounds. Continue around the 'farm' with cows (mooing), sheep (baaing), horses (neighing), dogs (barking), pigs (oinking) and hens (clucking). End the game with 'And then I was so tired I went home.' (The children lie down and pretend to fall asleep.)

obstacle course

Lay out a few items for the children to clamber over or wriggle under or through. You could try a large cushion, an open cardboard box, a play tunnel (if you have one), a small blanket and a beanbag.

copy me

Sit the children in a circle and ask them to copy your actions. Try clapping, waving, yawning and patting your tummy. End with them hiding their eyes and doing a peek-a-boo.

disco fun

Simply put on some lively music and all dance around altogether.

twinkle, twinkle, little star

This is one of the first rhymes most children learn. Get the children to open and close their hands like twinkling stars as you sing the words.

*Twinkle twinkle little star,
how I wonder what you are.
Up above the world so high,
like a diamond in the sky.
Twinkle, twinkle little star,
how I wonder what you are.*

Other great games for your two-year-old are:
- Happy birthday animals (see page 23)
- Five currant buns (see page 26)
- How do I dance? (see page 27)
- Hunt the teddy (see page 47)
- Make-believe animals (see page 51)
- Find the island (see page 51)
- What animal are you? (see page 58)
- Fishing pool (see page 60)
- Fluttering butterflies (see page 60)
- Frogs and fairies (see page 69)

the **3**rd birthday

B y the age of three, your child will probably have a small group of children she regularly plays with. Parties for this age tend to work best when it's just a small group of children – around six to eight is ideal – as they will still need close supervision and be easily prone to tears.

- At this stage children may find it difficult to cope with other children winning games or getting prizes. Stick to games that don't have a winner, or just applaud winners instead.

- If you do have prizes, have some tiny consolation prizes for children who haven't won.

- If you have shy guests, suggest they play with a partner.

- Some children will need their parents to stay, if only for a few minutes.

- The party's excitement can make children forget that they need to go to the toilet. Watch out for tell-tale signs.

great games

Here's a suggested list of games that are ideal for three-year-olds:

- If you're happy and you know it (see page 23)
- Five currant buns (see page 26)
- Clap my name (see page 33)
- The farmer's in his den (see page 33)
- Old MacDonald had a farm (see page 37)
- Pass the parcel (see page 41)
- Here we go round the mulberry bush (see page 40)
- Pat the balloon (see page 46)
- Hop, bunny, hop (see page 47)
- Traffic lights (see page 48)
- Flap the fish (see page 53)
- Fishing pool (see page 60)

safety

Three-year-olds are very mobile and love running around, so you'll need to be extra cautious about their safety, especially if their parents aren't staying. With the front door continually opening and closing, make sure no child accidentally runs out, or traps their fingers. Make a strict rule that the children may not open the door themselves to anyone. If you're concerned about three-year-olds banging doors, it's worth hanging a towel over the top to ensure it can't slam on any fingers.

Keep upstairs rooms out of bounds by closing the doors, and make sure the stairs are clear of any toys, coats or shoes. Put the guests' coats away in an upstairs room, so they don't clutter up the hall.

If you're planning to spend any time in the garden or outside, make sure your fences are secure and that any gates are locked. Put away any garden tools or chemicals and fence off or cover your pond – this is a safety essential for any parent, not just for a party.

If you have a lively pet you may want to consider asking a neighbour to look after him for a couple of hours, as many children are unused to animals and may be frightened – and your pet may find it upsetting too.

Oops!

It's inevitable that there will be spills at the tea table, so use an absorbent paper tablecloth (with a plastic one underneath to protect the table) and only half-fill the children's cups. If tea is going to be held on the carpet, you may want to buy cartons of drink with a straw instead.

Going home presents

From three onwards, your guests will be thrilled to have a party bag to take away. You don't have to fill this with expensive toys – a balloon, a piece of cake, a few sweets and a small plastic toy, such as a dinosaur, will be fine. Keep lollipops for party bags rather than party prizes, as the children will run around with the sticks in their mouths and this could be dangerous if they fall.

the **4**th birthday

B irthday parties are a key event for your four-year-old. She may already have been to several and will be anticipating her own with great excitement.

- By the age of four, children will have formed their own friendships, so involve your child in drawing up the party guest list.

- At the start of the party, give each child a name sticker. You may know all their names, but your helpers may not.

- Party clothes become quite important to children now, but make sure your child's outfit is comfortable. Have an extra layer she can put on or take off if she gets too cold or hot.

- If you're having a dressing-up party, send your invitations out well in advance to allow parents time to sort out a costume, or limit the outfit to just hats or funny masks.

- Remember to smile and look as if you're enjoying the party yourself – your attitude will rub off on the children.

great games

Here's a suggested list of games that are ideal for four-year-olds:
- Musical bumps (see page 25)
- Weird whispers (see page 32)
- In and out the dusty bluebells (see page 34)
- London Bridge is falling down (see page 38)
- Simon says (see page 45)
- Pat the balloon (see page 46)
- Find your partner (see page 46)
- Hunt the teddy (see page 47)
- Make-believe animals (see page 51)
- Bunny in the burrow (see page 58)

sorting out problems

No matter how well organized you are, there will be moments during the party when you feel the children are getting over-excited and silly. You will need to have a few strategies for coping with these situations.

Before you start the games, demonstrate a special sound to the children which means they've all got to 'freeze'. This could be a whistle, a bell or simply you saying 'Abracadabra!'. If things get out of hand you can use this fun device to stop the children in their tracks and switch over to a quieter game (see Chapter 5). Use this trick sparingly, otherwise the children will start to ignore it.

When you're choosing a child to start a new game, don't go for the one who is making the most noise. Say you'll pick someone who is sitting the most quietly and sensibly. It's amazing how effective this can be.

If one child is causing a problem, subtly ask an adult to join in the game alongside him to encourage him to play properly. If this doesn't work, try calling him over to you to be your 'helper'. Alternatively, end the lively game and begin a quiet one. As a last resort, ask an adult to take a disruptive child out of the room for some quiet time. Suggest that he can return when he's calmed down and warn him that he won't win any prizes while he's out. Don't ignore a potential problem, as it could spoil the other children's fun.

The tearful child

Parties can be an overwhelming experience for little ones and this is when your adult helpers become invaluable. Before the party, ask them to keep an eye out for children who are looking anxious and to anticipate tears before they happen.

If they do happen, kneel down to the child's eye level to ask what's wrong. She may simply need a big cuddle or someone to help her join in with the games. Alternatively, sit the tearful child with an adult helper who can read her a story until she feels better. If the tears don't stop, you may need to call her parents.

Going home presents

Four-year-olds love party bags, and will expect to get one by this stage. Interesting things to put in include:
- Mini pots of modelling clay
- Crayons
- Notepads
- Little play figures
- Hair clips or scrunchies
- Marbles
- Necklaces, bracelets, rings or clip-on jewellery
- Glider planes
- Pencil tops
- Bouncy balls
- Parachute toys
- Pirate eye patches

the **5**th birthday and beyond

You'll be well into the swing of parties by the time your child is five. From this age you may want to invite larger numbers – or even the whole class – and it's now that you may want to think about hiring an entertainer.

- This is probably the last year your child will want a mixed party, so make sure you have games and prizes for everyone.

- Children will be keen to inspect the contents of their party bag before they've even left, so hand it over as they leave.

- Don't embarrass anyone by assuming they can read – help them out as soon as you spot they're struggling.

- Put different toys into girls and boys party bags, as their tastes are very different at this age.

- Be firm about everyone remaining sitting down at the party tea.

great games

Here's a suggested list of games that are ideal for five-year-olds:
- Musical cushions (see page 25)
- Lost letter (see page 35)
- Squeak, Piggy, squeak! (see page 35)
- The chocolate game (see page 41)
- Limbo dancing (see page 44)
- Post-box race (see page 49)
- Sleepy lions (see page 56)
- Pin the tail on the piggy (see page 57)
- What's missing? (see page 57)
- What's in the box? (see page 59)

hiring an entertainer

Parents can feel very divided about the idea of hiring an entertainer. Some swear by it, saying it makes giving a party ten times easier; others say it's more friendly and fun to entertain the children yourself. Either way, it's an expensive option.

If you do decide to hire an entertainer, you can find one in your local telephone directory. However, a better way is to ask other parents if they can give you a personal recommendation. Ask if the entertainer worked well for the age group you're giving the party for, and what he cost.

Also check how long he entertains for – for instance will he do the whole two hours of a party, or just the hour before or after tea. If you can't get a personal recommendation, ask the entertainers you ring if they can pass on some phone numbers of previous clients and ring a couple to ask for their opinion.

As an alternative to an entertainer, you may want to take a small group of friends for a special birthday outing, perhaps to the cinema, a restaurant or theatre. This is particularly popular from the age of seven or eight up, as by this age your child usually has a small group of close friends and going out often makes them feel more grown-up.

Paint your own

A popular activity with over-fives is decorating their own biscuits or cakes with icing pens. Choose plain biscuits such as digestive, rich tea or finger biscuits and make sure you have enough pens for everyone. You may need to give a few suggestions, such as funny faces, their name, a spider's web or wavy patterns.

It's my party ...

... and I'll cry if I want to. And it's not unusual for the birthday boy or girl to get very overwrought and tearful towards the end of the party. Usually all that's needed is a drink and a cuddle from you in a quiet place away from the noise. Don't worry that your child hasn't enjoyed the party – he has, it's just all become too much for a moment.

index

Acknowledgments

Executive Editor Jane McIntosh
Editors Sharon Ashman and Joss Waterfall
Executive Art Editor Rozelle Bentheim
Designer Emily Wilkinson
Production Controller Viv Cracknell
Index compiled by Indexing Specialists